Sweet Sister Moon

Sweet Sister Moon

Poems by Norbert Krapf

WordTech Editions

Published by WordTech Editions
P.O. Box 541106
Cincinnati, OH 45254-1106

ISBN: 9781934999622
LCCN: 2009930077

Poetry Editor: Kevin Walzer
Business Editor: Lori Jareo

Visit us on the web at www.wordtechweb.com

Acknowledgments

The following poems originally appeared, sometimes in different from and with another title, in these publications: *Poetrybay* ("Sister Song," "Small Tombstone," "Still Born," "The Sister in the Circle"), *Confrontation* ("Seen from Behind," "In Bed"), *ELF: Eclectic Literary Forum* ("In Sheepskin," "Seated by a Tree"), *From the Edge of the Prairie* ("Lovely in Her Bones"), *Heartlands Today* ("In Black Velvet"), *Ixion.com* ("Against a Tree in Winter," "Seated on a Stool"), *Long Island Quarterly* ("Helga Asleep," "In Braids," "On Her Back," "She Daydreams"), *Poems That Thump in the Dark* ("Behind Drawn Shades"), *Poetz.com* ("Soul Song"), *SpinDrifter* ("The Figure in the Landscape," "Blues Valentine," "Woods Shrine"), *Valparaiso Poetry Review* ("Still Dark"), *Willow Springs* ("Seated on a Stool"). Thanks to the editors for permission to reprint.

"Southern Girl in Snowstorm," "Preservation," "Daughter," "When the Call Came," "Elizabeth Maria's Colombian Eyes," "Stars," and "After Love" are reprinted from the author's *Bittersweet Along the Expressway: Poems of Long Island* (Waterline Books, 2000), copyright © 2000 Norbert Krapf; "Sisters" appeared in *Somewhere in Southern Indiana: Poems of Midwestern Origins,* copyright © 1993 Time Being Books, and is reprinted by permission of Time Being Books; "Hugging the Spirit," "On the Road with the Hampton Sisters," "Sister Query," "Song for a Sister," and "What Have You Gone and Done?" appeared in *Bloodroot: Indiana Poems* (2008), copyright © Indiana University Press, and are reprinted by permission; the second and fifth poems just listed, as well as "Girl of the Hill Country" and "The Other Side," appeared on the CD with pianist and composer Monika Herzig, *Imagine – Indiana in Music and Words* (Acme Records, 2007), paired with her compositions or arrangements of traditional jazz tunes.

"Song for Cassandra Wilson" appeared in the booklet series *Dancing to the Music of Poetry 9* (Feral Press, 2004), edited by Joan and John Digby. "The Riddle of Three Words" originally appeared in *Family Celebrations: Prayers, Poems, and Toasts for Every Occasion* (Andrews McMeel Publishing,

1999), edited by June Cotner, and was reprinted in the anthologies *To Love One Another: Poems Celebrating Marriage* (Grayson Books, 2002) and *Proposing on the Brooklyn Bridge: Poems About Marriage* (Grayson Books, 2003), both edited by Ginny Lowe Connors. "Angel Sister Song" first appeared in the "Airpoets" anthology *Rivers, Rails, and Runways* (2008) and is reprinted by permission of San Francisco Bay Press.

Thanks to Jeanetta Calhoun for the poem "Goddess" in *Tongue Tied Woman* (Sarasota Theater Press, 2001), the trigger for some of these poems; to Kriss Luckett-Ziesemer for her song, as sung with Greg Ziesemer, for the epigraph, the book's title, and the inspiration for "Full Moon Over Central Indiana"; to Monika Herzig for her invitation to combine poetry and jazz; to the other Indiana musicians the author has had the pleasure of working with, including Tim Grimm and Gordon Bonham; to Karen Kovacik for listening to Ramona and daring to speak back; to the "Airpoets" of Central Indiana, Joyce Brinkman, Ruthelen Burns, Joseph Heithaus, and Jeannie Deeter Smith, for their critiques; and to Ashley Verkamp of the author's native Dubois County, Indiana, for creating the cover art on commission.

For Dorothy,
Mary, and Marilyn,
(born Jan. 25, 1950,
died Jan. 25, 1950),

Klara, 1869-1943,

Katherine,
Elizabeth, and Christie,

and the larger family
of sisters and daughters

When she returns, it is always summer.
Don't you hear the swallows and cicadas?
Don't you hear the nightingale?
Don't you hear the brooks running silver,
the rivers running darkly to the sea?
Don't you hear the whole world singing
her praises? Everything is singing, everyone
is in love, because our goddess has come home.
            –Homer, "Hymn to Aphrodite"
             adapted by Patricia Monoghan

 I keep your flowers safe in my pocket
Tucked away for some rainy night
When I'm feelin' all small and round
Like you, like you tonight
My sweet sister moon
Oh, my sweet sister moon.
            –Kriss Luckett-Ziesemer,"Sweet Sister Moon"
             from the Diamonds & Rust CD *Bitterskin*

The Spirit of the Fountain dies not.
It is called the Mysterious Feminine.
The Doorway of the Mysterious Feminine
Is called the Root of Heaven-and-Earth.

Lingering like gossamer, it has only a hint of existence;
And yet when you draw upon it, it is inexhaustible.
            –Lao Tzu, *Tao Teh Ching*
             Tr. John C.H. Wu

Table of Contents

1. The Figure in the Landscape

The Figure in the Landscape

I found my goddess
in the lay of the land
I love, in the curves

of her rolling hills,
the rise and spread
of trees in her woods,

in the tangle of
weeds and wildflowers
that grow lush

in her fallow fields,
in the way she
opens herself to rain

and accepts the snow
and swells and heaves
in the hot sun.

When I tongue
the names shagbark
hickory and white oak,

sycamore and sweet
gum, beech, black
cherry and walnut;

prairie grass, Queen
Anne's lace, mullein
and blackberries,

sassafras, pawpaw
persimmon, pecan
and tulip poplar;

Dutchman's breeches,
bloodroot, May apple,
and wild geranium;

and voice the names
of those who came
before me and mine,

Miami, Piankashaw,
Lenape, Shawnee
Wea and Potawatomi,

I feel my goddess
listen and respond
to my naming

and know she
welcomes me back
to the land I love.

Woods Shrine

When my father led me as a boy
into the woods beyond the old
farmhouse near the top of the hill
at the end of the red sandstone lane

I did not know you were waiting
but I sensed a presence in the woods
I did not perceive anywhere else.
For the first time, I carried a rifle

on my shoulder as we hunted squirrels.
All my senses entered a new dimension.
Eyes, ears detected every range of motion,
every nuance of sound. Now I know

you were there waiting for an acolyte.
Now I know you were preparing me
for what would come later. Silently,
skillfully you led me toward your depths.

When I tiptoed around the base of one
food tree, you backed around another.
When I ran my fingertips up and down
the smooth bark of a beech, your skin

tingled but you kept your pleasure to
yourself. I had not found the capacity
to name what I loved, never heard
the name that other men gave you,

and so I did not know to say, "Daphne!"
When I squinted at the early morning
sunlight that sometimes broke through
a cluster of leaves, I did not know

it was light from your heavenly eyes.
Now when I lie with you as morning
light filters through the blinds and you
prepare to rise and depart, I recall

where I saw that familiar light so long
ago and so far away. Goddess of leaf,
branch, bole, and bark, your devotee is back.
I have returned to the shade of your shrine.

Lovely in Her Bones

after Theodore Roethke

I once knew a woman so lovely
in her bones I followed her down
the lane past the river into a field
where monarchs fluttered in clouds.

The woman who moved so grace-
fully in her bones through milkweed
and Queen Anne's lace turned
around, bowed like a violinist
who has made ethereal music,
touched her fingertips to lips,
gave me a gracious wave,
tiptoed like a fawn into shadowy
woods where pawpaws grow
and mourning doves coo
sad songs one after another.

As butterflies touched my flesh
like blessings from beyond
I gave thanks for what I had
been allowed to behold

and wrote down this prayer
so the woman divine in her
flesh may come back
to this world again because
she knows how grateful I am
she has walked down my lane,
stood in my field, shone the light
of her grace, and blessed me
with the power to say what
I feel by the way she walks
so lovely in her bones.

Girl of the Hill Country

after Bob Dylan and traditional song

 If you're traveling in the hill country
where woods roll as far as you can see
and the sun sets on the hazy Ohio River,
say hello to a girl I once loved.

Tell her I remember that wisp of hair
that trailed across big blue eyes,
the way she would say my name
with a voice that rose like a spring.

If you see snowflakes pile on cedar green,
tell me if she still wears that same smile
that makes winter skin tingle when
blood flows oh so slow in your veins.

If you see the old red barns lean
in heat where purple hollyhocks stand,
please ask if she remembers my name,
tell her I dream of coming back home.

If you're traveling in the hill country
when yellow leaves fall, remember me
to one who lives there. My lips still
hold the sound of her name like a hymn.

Insomniac's Aubade

Old flame, you come again.
How could I ever say no?

You know just where
to put your toes on the stairs
so they do not creak, tiptoe
so deftly into the bedroom,
let your gown slip to the floor
like leaves falling in a breeze.
Only I feel them land on the carpet.

The mattress barely moves
as you lie down beside me,
breathe on my lips. How do
I know in the dark the color
of your eyes and soft hair?
Your full lips are moist
like earth after spring rain.

Without a single word
we move into one another,
cling together like dancers
who know every inch of the floor,
when to lead, when to follow.

After we have built
and spent our need,
we relax and move apart,
but the pods of our
little fingers continue
to touch for hours
as we stare together
at the invisible ceiling.

Just before birds begin
to stitch their song
and gray threads through
the blinds, you rise like mist
without saying good-bye.

Shoveling Snow in Moonlight

At a time when she often comes
to make poems revolve in my mind,

the full moon and the glow of heavy
snow pull me up and out of bed.

I step outside in boots and begin to
shovel snow in moonlight. Hours later

sunlight finds me still lifting,
stacking, re-arranging wet snow.

When the back door opens, I trudge into
the house to wish my wife happy birthday

and must agree I stayed out too long.
But wasn't there something redeeming

in the physical labor in the quietest
hour of the morning? a familiar voice

asks me. *Like chopping wood? Like*
feeding the cows? Well, yes, I have

to concede. *I think the muse needs*
some physical exercise now and then,

the voice concludes. But not so intense
that she becomes worn out, I want to say.

I want her to come back refreshed,
in moonlight or sunshine, again and again.

Blues Valentine

Sock it to me, woman from above,
come on back down to this earth,
come on down to my loving level,
give me your sultry smoky lines,
lay your red-hot images up
and down my waiting flesh,
tattoo me with red and blue hearts,
breathe your steamy somethings
into my unstopped ears,
rock me mama, ride me high
in your free-style rhythms, take me
all the way with your organic form
right on home to the roadhouse
jumping under moss-hung live oaks,
throw away the road map and the rules,
yeah, light my literary fire under
the full moon, my mystical muse,
do a slow country dance with me,
boogie me out onto Highway 61,
come on back home with me,
give me voice, give me flame,
give me the power of your vision
to sing a hymn of praise to your love.

Memo of Understanding

I know, woman of the night,
you must also be with other
men and women. I vow
not to make a singular claim
on your expansive affection
nor circumscribe your gift.

But when you come in the dark
you must give all of yourself,
human and divine, to move me
beyond my limits, as I must
give all of my mortal self
to you. In this we must
be true, never compromise.

After we share the epiphany
of love that moves me to expression,
let lips and tongues touch goodbye,
I shall not ask where you go
nor when you shall return.

But woman of luminous eyes
that enlarge my vision
and warm breath that lifts
my voice to the depths,
do not glance back to see
where I go or what I do
under cover of daylight.
What we give and take,
my shadowy love, lives
and dies only in the dark.

Her Gift

What I love
is not what
we say but
what we do not
have to say.

What I love
is what you
know, do not
say, but
mysteriously
give to me
to say.

Soul Song

When our lips touched,
hers were so soft
and moist mine opened,

and I felt her soul slip in
and tingle the tongue that
gives you these words.

Tongues of Fire

When holy fire
wings down
from beyond

tongue sends streams
of words sparking
into dumb dark

like shooting stars
pilgrims may follow.
When tongue turns

into instrument
of love it seeks
and finds seams

and folds of flesh
to ignite into
another kind of

flame that leaps
along circuits
of feeling.

When tongue
comes as Paraclete
and instrument

of love at once,
devotees assemble
and fires burn

throughout groves
as spirit and flesh
sing for all time.

2. Woman in a Lavender Field

Love Song in the Kitchen

My bedroom hung
right above her kitchen.
I woke to the hum
of her bustle,
her ongoing song
of family life.

When she was a girl,
she lay on corn shucks
with her sister
in the upstairs bedroom,
gazing at stars through
cracks in the roof.

Sometimes a snowflake
fell on her face.

She liked to hear
her daddy pluck
the mandolin
and sing tenor.

His music stopped
when she was six,
except in her mind.

She still hums
his country song
in my kitchen.
Snowflakes fall
on my face.

Emily Dickinson's Loaves

In her mother's kitchen
Emily kneaded the dough
and shaped it into loaves

and let them rise as she
tiptoed up the stairs
to her bedroom and took

out a piece of blank paper
and with flour on fingertips
she scratched out a poem

that rose from the depths.
When it was finished
she slipped it into a drawer,

sneaked back down the stairs,
put the loaves into the oven
and let the bread bake

as she climbed back up the stairs
in a white dress, another poem
swelling inside her. When it

rose she traced it in ink on paper
and put the sheet on the pile
expanding inside the drawer.

Sometimes when she wrote
she felt flour on her fingers
and sometimes when she ate

a slice of bread she tasted
the tang of poems on her tongue.
When Emily died, sister Lavinia

tiptoed into her bedroom
where the chest of drawers
glowed in the sun like an oven

and opened the drawers
and found loaves of poems
baked to perfection

giving off the smell
of daredevil courage
and indomitable spirit.

Hugging the Spirit

Odysseus followed Circe's advice,
sailed north into cold shadows,
offered warm blood to raise the spirits.

Thus he found his mother, who had died
while he wandered. He longed to hug her,
to hold her close, but could not reach her,

whom he loved so much, whose voice
spoke his name across the abyss. For even
when spirit is as close as the heartbeat

in your chest, you cannot reach out
and touch it. You must honor the distance,
even as you feel the pulse of the cord.

So I flew back home, Mother, and found you
in your reclining chair in the corner of the room
where morning light enters. You rose, shakily,

out of the shadows. I put my arms around
what I could find of you, held what was left
of your flesh, and kissed your thinning lips.

It was like kissing the mist in the valleys.
I saw faint light flicker in your sunken eyes.
I knew I could not hold you for long.

I had to let you return to the shadows.
I sat and watched you labor to breathe
with your eyes closed. I played a tape

I made of songs you loved, in the old tongue.
I saw your lips shape some of the words.
Once you voiced a line in a high register,

and almost smiled. I knew you were sailing
back to rejoin the father who died when
you were but a little girl. It was as clear

as the sunlight that you were ready to go.
I tried not to hold on too long, for I knew
that spirit cannot be contained in one world.

Love Story

A woman thought
she fell in love
with a man.

After a time
they decided they
liked one another

but the relationship
had come as far
as it could go.

They would take
a break to see
what might happen.

Then the man's
brother, who had
admired the woman,

asked permission
of his brother
to date the woman.

The woman fell
in love with this
other brother.

They got married
and the first man
came to the wedding.

In nine months
a son was born
who later wrote

a poem to tell
how you go about
finding the right

father as well as
an uncle who is
tender to his nephew.

Letter to You

Maybe you are
the blue-eyed girl
with the warm smile
I was to marry
but did not because
you sensed we were
too young, you didn't
know where you were
going with your life,
and had to put a crack
in my heart, though
you didn't want to,
because that was
the only way you
could get to where
you needed to move.

Maybe you are
the sister I almost had
but did not because you
died just when you were
born yet somehow became
a part of the sister who
did stay in this world
and is such a friend.

Maybe you are
the blonde German girl
with moss-green eyes
who lived in our house
as my daughter several
months, played the violin
with such soul, and after
you left disappeared
into a clinic and never
wrote back even though

you got out, because you
could not find the words
to explain what happened.

Maybe you are
the daughter who was
never born but became
a part of the beautiful
dark-eyed baby who
came to us wrapped
in a multicolored blanket
in the arms of a slender,
long-haired Colombian girl
who handed you to us
in Kennedy Airport.

Maybe you are
the woman who was
such a good mother
to me but had to leave
for the world of spirit
where I will one day
find you again.

Maybe you are
the quiet young woman
who was in my class, smiled
with such understanding,
wrote so well about
literature, touched me
on the arm when the term
was over, said thanks,
touched her lips to mine.

Maybe you are
the Jewish woman
with my last name who
died in Theresienstadt

but came back to life
in the poems I sang
in your memory
and speaks to me
like a sister now
in e-mails I receive
from your relative
on the other coast
of North America.

Maybe you are
one or all of these
and if you are
you knew before I did
what I wanted to say
but don't have to.

Ripples

for Sandy Jahmi Burg

When a rock skips over
the water in a reservoir
and settles down into
the depths we cannot fathom,
ripples spread wider and wider
on the surface we watch.

When the sounds of creatures
hidden in the woods where
we stand stop, ripples of silence
circle around us and lift us
to new levels of intensity.

When someone we love
moves on, ripples pass
through us, from one
to another, and beyond us,

and we do not know
how far or how long
they will spread
or lead us, but we
feel ourselves lean
in a direction we
did not know we
could ever take.

May Day Song

Not far from where
the male dove coos,

the coy female sits
facing the other way,

her fine ears opening
like blossoms in the sun.

The Riddle of Three Words

When you think
you have found
the right person
to say them to

you must make sure
you mean them
with all your life
and have earned
the right to say them.

You must also wonder
if the other will
believe and accept them.

Mere volume will not
convince either of you.

If you hear them
said to you
you must wonder
if they are truly meant,
if you are indeed
the one for whom
they are intended,
if you deserve them,
and exactly what they mean.

If these conditions
are all satisfied
and you can say
and receive them
in all faith

they will seem
the most beautiful
short poem
in any language

and you will pray
you may say
and hear it
every day
the rest
of your life.

Southern Girl in Snowstorm

She rushes outside
as though she's found

the first ripe vegetable
in a new winter garden.

Her hands cup enough
fluff to press together

into a whiffle ball that
flutters back into her face

when she lobs it
into the north wind.

She stoops and rubs
the cold white cream

onto tingling red cheeks.
Her mittens are strawberry

Popsicles, her boots
a pair of tropical black

animals suffering across
the tundra. She flops

to her bottom and toboggans
down the silver sidewalk.

Back inside, she shucks
off layers of wool and wilts

by a radiator like an indoor
plant exposed to first frost.

Early Morning Love Song

Kiss me
on my early
morning lips

and you
are my muse
forever.

After Love

In the first
light of this
day that opened
so beautifully

I look out
the window and
see the birch
by the garage

naked of leaves
twisting a fine
torso, stretching
white arms and

throwing hair-
fine branches
forward as if
rising from

a night of sleep
and love and
yawning in
satisfaction

Woman in a Lavender Field

You might not believe this,
but a woman is filling a wicker
basket with fragrant sprigs
of lavender in a field
in flat central Indiana.

The sun is bright,
the air is clear, the sky
is blue, not along
the Mediterranean,
but in a field on a farm
in central Indiana.

The woman, who sits
on the ground in a straw hat
beside a luxuriant bush
of lavender, smiles in the sun
beside her basket, in which
rubber bands wrap around
200 fresh lavender spikes.

You might think rows
of different varieties of lavender
would not grow, certainly
not so elegantly, in a plain
place like central Indiana.

You may be thinking
of the south of France,
where Mediterranean sun
illuminates the landscape
the whole day long
and the singing sea
washes the shore beside
which the woman sits,

but I tell you this harvest
of lavender was picked
on a small farm in land-locked
central Indiana in a flat
and out-of-the-way field
you would not consider
worth searching out.

As if in partial concession,
the woman's smile implies
she may have pulled off
the unexpected: to harvest,
almost by herself, this
bounty of beauty to the eye,
this blessing of fragrance,
in a place where almost nobody
would believe such a delight
could grow or be found.

But let me confess:
the scent of lavender
comes off my fingertips,
the feel of warm sun
is on the nape of my neck,
I picked almost half
the lavender in the basket,
which is woven with
matching purple strands,
and I sing this song
of a wife who found
unexpected delight in a field
where the usual skeptics
would not bother to tread
though angel tracks abound.

Preservation

You sit on the floor
  in front of the fire
    and pull the frayed edges

    of a rose, royal blue,
  and beige oriental rug
onto your lap. The black

and white kitten that
  was thrown from a car
    into the ivy in front

    of the house rolls
  in the folds between
you and the fire rubbing

belly and back against
  birds swaying on stalks
    of irises in bloom.

    With needle and thread
  you stitch together strips
of a woolen rug shredded

by a machine, swab
  light spots with left-
    over coffee to darken

    the background. As I
  poke at the logs flickering
on the andirons you rescued

from the refuse
  in front of an antique
    shop, you rub a finger

between the kitten's
oversized ears and say: *I love
to save what other people throw away.*

3. The Sister in the Circle

Sisters

1
My first sister
was born without
ever drawing a
breath. I heard
my mother cry
and my grandmother
scold her upstairs.

2
When my second sister
began to cry,
my mother breathed
a lot easier. My
grandmother smiled.
The dolls we kept
clapped their hands.

Song for a Sister

Back at the site of your tiny tomb,
sister, still not sure what to say.

First fact: Born Jan. 25, 1950.
Second fact: Died Jan. 25, 1950.
This year you would
have turned forty-five.

They named you Marilyn,
but you may have been gone
by the time the name was given.
Or perhaps the name was selected
and waiting like a baptismal
gown sewn for you to fit into.

I don't know whether to say
you died in being born
or were already dead
before you could be born.

Let's just say your death
coincided with your birth
and that I never saw you.

I believe in you nonetheless.
Perhaps I miss you more
for never having met you.

Whenever I return from
the Island in the East
I come back to your small
stone on which it is carved:
GONE TO BE AN ANGEL.

Halcyon times, the time

of your birth and death,
the pundits tell us,
but I remember our mother's
grief all too well, the sound
of her sobs descending the stairs
from the bedroom in which
her mother scolded her hard.

Grandma's husband, you may know,
left her and this world at age thirty-three
with six young children on the farm.
No time for self-pity. Pigs to feed
and butcher. Meals to cook,
clothes to wash, crops to put in.

Our father swallowed his grief
over the loss of a daughter,
carried it for years.
It had to tear at his guts.

Marilyn, I have concluded
that in talking to you
I speak to that part of myself
I have not been lucky enough
to discover but which will one
day rejoin and complete me.

The green grass of summer
grows around your clean-carved,
well-trimmed tombstone
not far from the tall tomb
of the maternal ancestor
who came from Lohr am Main.

To return here
from far away
and try to preserve
even the slightest trace

of you is to pay
tribute to a life so dear
its mysterious end
arrived as it began.

Sister Query

for Marilyn

What does it mean, sister, to die
as you are born? Were you never
alive in our mother's womb?

Did you never draw one breath
in this or any other world? Is
there no one but me who knows

you were and still are there?
Am I the single believer in this
religion of one with you as

center and source of my creed?
Are all those I love in this realm
doubting Thomases when it comes

to you and your invisible life?
Is it your breath I hear
and sometimes feel in the night

when everyone else sleeps?
Will I one day wake to look
into your soulful eyes that have

looked at me across this divide
since I was born? Could you
be alive on the other side

and I have been stillborn in this
realm apart from you and those
who left here to join with you?

Will I one day see the light
in your eyes wherever they
went before they could open

and walk with you however
you have walked since the day
you were born and died

in the same moment
in and out of whatever
world is still mine?

Sister Song

Oh sis
when you came
into and left this
world without
ever drawing
a breath I felt
a tremor
in the house
and sadness hung
for years like
smoke beneath
the kitchen ceiling
until another sister
came and stayed

and ever since
that day of
your birth and death
I have felt around
the world like
a blind brother
to touch you
and bring you back.

Angel Sister Song

1
Marilyn, Marilyn, sister
I never saw or heard,
I say your name to summon
you back into this world
they say you never were in,
because you were born dead.
Those who see it so are
unborn into your presence.

2
Born dead, born still,
means you always
were spirit, oh my sister
born dead. Never flesh,
always spirit, born dead,
born still, you live
for me outside time,
oh sister stillborn.

3
Speak, sister, speak.
For decades I've been
training these ears to hear
the voice of an angel
who never found a home
in flesh. Sing, sister,
sing in spirit breath.

4
Teach me, Marilyn,
to sing a song that will
wing me into your world
that waits beyond
the one in which I live.

Angel sister, breathe
spirit song in my ear.

Still Born?

Does it mean
you were silent
when you died
the moment
of your birth

or that sixty
years after you
died you are
still busy
being born?

Small Tombstone

Stillborn sister
lies on her back
staring into eternity.

Still Dark

It was still dark
when I rose
in the town

where I was born
but have not lived
for fifty years

and dressed
and followed my
feet to the large

sandstone church
and the open gate
into the old cemetery

and crunched down
the white gravel lane
past the large stone

crucifix marking
the grave of the
Croatian missionary

priest who brought
German Catholics
into these hills

a hundred years
before your birth
and untimely death;

past the tombstone
carved in German
script honoring

the ancestor who died
only three years after he
and his wife and their

six Kinder arrived;
veered slightly to
the left as a hint

of gray appeared
over my head;
stopped at the third

row of tiny tombstones
and moved into
the damp grass

to find the small
granite stone third
in from the lane;

and waited for light
to find your name,
Marilyn Krapf,
daughter of Dorothy
and Clarence,
and the lettering,

carved to endure,
of the single date
that tells the story

and confirms
the mystery
of your birth

January 25,
1950, co-

inciding

with your
death, January
25, 1950,

oh my sister
I will never
forget.

The Sister in the Circle

If there is a circle
will it still be unbroken
when I come inside?

Are you still waiting,
my sister stillborn,
inside the circle?

Are you connected
inside the circle
to mother and father?

Will the circle inside
of which we come together
be unbroken for all time?

Has it been you I've been
hearing all these years
calling me to come home?

4. Daughters

Daughter

On dark winter nights,
between the sighing of steam
from radiators, I have heard
your breath slip beneath
the door and fill up the bedroom
like a balloon which deflated
at the break of day.

Sometimes I have cradled you
in my arms before the fireplace
and rocked you asleep as logs
crumbled through the grate.

Coming home from work
I have tiptoed up the stairs
to find you still breathing
in the antique cradle
in the guest bedroom, stooped
over, and kissed you awake.

But your toys never littered
my study, your diapers never
fouled my bathroom. I never
held my breath through your
routine sicknesses, never had
to wonder how I would endure
your growing into the woman
some strange man would
take from my house.

But I have felt you,
daughter, when the children
of those I love hugged me.
I see your lines in their
bright drawings I tape

to the refrigerator door,
hear your voice rise
in their chatter.

Ah, my daughter, I can
almost feel you reading
over my shoulder as I write.
Your harsh cry would have
been music to my night.

When the Call Came

When the call came
I was about to cut the grass
for the first time. Wild
onion and dandelion were
sprouting across the lawn.
Sheaths of lily of the valley
bearing round green bells
were surrounding the lilac.

When the call came
the yellow marsh marigolds
were rising like the sun
against a boulder in
the flower bed. Bees
buzzed around bunches
of purple grape hyacinth.
The operator said, *I have
a collect call from Colombia.
Do you accept the charges*?
I replied, *Yes, I accept.*

When the call came
the leathery leaves
of bloodroot along the ledge
of the stone wall were
wrapped around stalks
like green sheets on which
white petals lay. Beside
the fishpond the fronds
of maidenhair fern were
unfurling in the sun.
A voice with a Spanish
accent spoke in my ear,
*This is a social worker. We
have a baby girl born eight*

days ago. Will you accept her?

When the call came
the white blossoms
of the wild cherry at the edge
of the woods were fluttering
on black boughs. The tips
of Japanese irises were
pushing through the soil.
Specks of Bibb lettuce
lay like green confetti
on the upper level of
the rock garden. *Yes, we
accept her,* I said. *Yes.*

Elizabeth Maria's
Colombian Eyes

Twin moons
of tropi-
cal night

daylight
breaking
through.

Stars

Where our daughter
stoops and sniffs

beneath maple saplings
along the wire fence

tiny cluster-rays
of aster violet

beam out of
the darkening green.

Sweet Sixteen

For your sixteenth birthday
I let you pick out a necklace
at the Thunderbird Coffee & Gift
Shop at the edge of the reservation.

With impeccable taste you select
a white bone and pink shell choker
with leather tie made by a Shinnecock
artist. Later I find matching earrings
and slip them into the bag.

On your birthday, you tie
on the choker, insert earrings,
and give a regal smile.

Your ebony Colombian eyes
shine, your dark hair catches
the light, your nostrils flare
slightly, the coffee and cream
skin of your face and neck
set off the Shinnecock choker
and earrings perfectly.
Who is this exotic queen
with such sensual lips
just turned sweet sixteen?

When I raise the camera
to capture the moment,
you do not fear, like some
of your ancestors would have,
that I am stealing your soul.
The way that you smile says
you know you are loved.

When a few days later
we look together at the print
I say the bone and shell
choker and earrings
make you more beautiful.
"Daddy," you conclude, "they
bring out the Indian in me."
Yes, daughter of earth and air
who descended from the Andes
to settle into our man-made house.

Consolation Song for a Daughter

When the first girl
I ever fell in love with
and who promised me
she would be my wife
told me we would
have to break up,
the pain was unbearable
even though I had sensed
what was coming.

I did not care
what kind of sun
was supposed to rise.

But to be blind-sided
by the young man you
thought would stay
at your side for the duration
must have come as pure
devastation. He was not
wrong to realize that his
life had not ripened enough
to join with yours.

One day a man will emerge
who will perceive that
the light shining through
your dark Colombian eyes
comes from a source
beyond where we live
and that such beauty
requires a devotion
and dedication that
will make him become

the human being whose
strength of spirit
will help him realize
that the gift which
you are will fulfill
the potential he has.

A Bruch Concerto in the Basement

for Natascha Kutscher, 17

It begins as a warm-up,
as mere exercise,
as three-octave scale
straightforward at first,
then in different rhythms,
becomes double stops in thirds,
takes on a warmer tone
as notes slur sensually.

Then, as if breaking through
the ceiling into another dimension,
it touches you in the living room
above where you sit reading
a book whose pages stay still

as it deepens into a rich
lyric run in the great concerto
carrying more and more feeling
as it climbs higher and higher
until it reaches a point
almost beyond her grasp,
then releases into the pause
of an extended vibrato....

My ear leads my eye
to see the dark-brown
eighteenth-century violin
clasped against the fair
skin of her graceful neck,
the long blonde hair falling
over her shoulders, the focus
of her moss-green eyes
as the curved fingers hold

the bow that moves horsehair
across steel strings to make
this magical pattern of sound

and you marvel at
the mystery of love
that brought her into
this world to parents
in the country where
your ancestors lived until
a century and a half ago

to become now a sister
to your daughter practicing
viola in her bedroom upstairs,
second sister to your son
picking and strumming a guitar
in the bedroom next door,
second daughter to your wife
stirring food at the stove,
gift of a second daughter
to you who received the first
as more miracle than he
ever dared to expect.

Acoma Wedding Vase

for Elizabeth and Chris

When you hold this clay vase
in warm hands, you may think
you feel the beat of one heart
with two arteries open at the top.

You must learn whether
to believe and trust what you feel
and think about one another
and how to balance thought and feeling

as they lead you on the winding road
you hope may lead to the home that,
lit by a candle that never goes out,
all couples past, present and future,

yearn to find. Into this wedding vase
I would pour a special medicine
of herbal oils, fruitful distillations,
and elements according to a recipe

passed down by one generation
to another and ask you to place
each a finger on the bridge
connecting one ventricle to

the other, lift the heart in balance,
and sip in turn from either side
a potion that will give you
the patience to find the right

mix to carry you and those who
descend from you the love that
heals, strengthens, and sustains
making all Spirit and time one.

Walt Whitman's Daughters

for Shakira Acosta and Christie Cooke

On an eleventh-month afternoon
on Paumanok we trade impressions
of Walt nurturing a runaway slave
and juxtaposing that episode
with the incident of a well-to-do
woman hiding behind the curtains
of her fine house while in her fantasies
she gives herself to twenty-eight
young men splashing in the salt
water not far beyond her window

and I look up from my text
and see across the desk from me
two young women, one Puerto Rican,
one Navajo, their dark eyes ablaze,
one pair round as full moons,
the other parallel ripe almonds,
huddling together close as sisters
brought together by kindred spirits
and the distance from their homes

and I understand better than ever
before how a kelson of the creation
is indeed love and that all men
and women are brothers and sisters
and that a man is rich in proportion
to the number of daughters and sons
he can admit into his affection
and carry with him as he journeys forth
every day the rest of his life

and I, a native Midwesterner,
conclude that a country

that can produce a poet like
Walt Whitman from an Island
off the East Coast who brings us
together to share our perceptions
from different perspectives
and bloodlines and places
so far apart in so many ways
is richer than I ever imagined.

Beyond Dark Eyes:
A Navajo Cycle

for Christie Cooke

1. Diné Degree

When you climb these Eastern
steps to the stage in buckskin
moccasins, woven black
and red rug dress, turquoise
and silver squash blossom
necklace that your grandmother
once wore and the sliver concha
belt that once wrapped around
the waist of another woman in your
family many come with you

and when you walk in such beauty
across the hardwood floor
to receive your certificate
and have your picture taken
all those who came before walk
in beauty, light shining in dark eyes,

and although you are
the very first in your family
to take this particular walk
you know you shall
not be the last

for when one Navajo
walks in beauty all Navajos
past, present and future
walk with her and many
shall follow in your graceful
footsteps and you shall lead

sisters and brothers and daughters
and sons to walk in balance
up a series of steps

and one day you shall
turn to look back and see
a long line of Diné people
who descend from you
as well as your mother
and father and grandmother
and grandfather and their
ancestors walking in beauty
behind you and they
shall be looking up to you
singing your name
in a hymn of praise
that will bless all who
follow in your footsteps.

2. Diné Daughter

walks upright, keeps her
dark eyes wide open,
speaks only when she is
moved to the right words.
Sometimes she is twenty-one,
sometimes she is fifty-one.
The press of her foot to sandy
earth springs a hundred affections.
White evening primroses blossom
at her feet and blue sky opens
above her head. When she
walks she moves with the grace
of water that finds its own channel
and swirls in the right place.
Her wrists are thin but her
hands are strong and the touch

of her fingertips tells you
what she feels about you.
Her Navajo natural voice
is gentle but she can be
as strong as wind when it
shifts and rises to righteous
anger whipped up by what
is wrong. Her rich brown
skin darkens in the sun
and her raven hair gives
off black radiance when
she lets it fall down.
When she is with her
brothers and sisters she
giggles like a little girl
and nieces and nephews
crawl into her lap for hugs
and kisses. Her mother
and father smile more
when she is in their house.
When she is outside the circle
of the Four Sacred Mountains
she carries Dinétah in her big
heart and corn pollen in her
small handbag. No matter
how far she is from her
homeland the old stories
of her father and the warm
wisdom of her mother keep
her spirit calm and strong
and make her confident she
can do whatever her heart wills.
When she hugs you goodbye,
Diné daughter lets you feel
how much you mean to her
and reminds you that
the faith you have in her
is the best investment

your heart can make.

3. On the Rim

Grand Canyon

She sits down
on a shelf of
rock on the overlook,
folds in her legs,
leans forward,
rests chin on rail,
and gazes into
the expanse below,
and far beyond.

Nothing you can see
of her moves, not
even her eyes.

Poised between heavens
and earth, between past,
present and future,
she looks out from
within herself and her
heritage and perceives
gradations of red
and brown earth,
patches of blue-green
vegetation clinging
to cliffs, dark green
of river bending between
shadows of valley.

A hawk soaring in
currents glides by
close to her shoulder

and raven dark hair
and cries out a ritual
greeting in language
darker than her
earth-brown skin.

What she sees
she keeps to
herself to carry
forth and let ripen
into language that
will bless those
who came before
as they move forward
into those who follow

and consecrate
the creation she
loves and shall
leave behind.

4. Female Hogan

Monument Valley

Inside the female hogan
where everything is round
and meets in the center
you explain to your teacher
that inside a hogan one
must always walk
in the right direction
as the sun and seasons
and all life move,
and that as a child
you were punished for
walking the wrong way.

Teacher turned student knows
you have learned to take your
own steps in the right direction,
has seen you walk in balance
with a grace all your own,

knows any man who
would walk with you
and join his life with yours
at the center must be able
to take the right steps
in the direction you
have discovered
and measure his stride
in rhythm with yours.

Your teacher puts a hand
on your strong yet tender
shoulder, allows a finger
to touch the soft flesh
at the base of your neck,

looks out the entrance
toward the East, feels
the West tug at his back,
wants to pull you toward
him, but knows he must
learn to let you go
wherever heart's push
and pull will take you.

5. New Old Tongue

Canyon de Chelly

When you let yourself

go down layer by layer
of generations through
what some call time
you shall feel
the beautiful black bird
of the ancient tongue
flap its wings and rise
from the branches
of a tall tree to meet
you and give you
a power that surges
through your spirit
and your outstretched
wings shall catch currents
and you shall climb
to where you have
never been until you
burst into sunlight
and soar and cry out
in a new old tongue
and everything that lives,
dies and is reborn
in the canyon below
shall look up and listen
and follow wherever
you glide and go.

6. Night Vision

Below white walls
against white sheets
in the dark

a thick mane
of black hair
covers most of

her round face
and when she
turns her head

slowly in deep
sleep her hair
falls gracefully

away from her
forehead and eyelids
revealing a face

that glows in
beauty while I
lie in the dark

one bed away
inhaling and exhaling
a prayer of praise.

7. Eastern Light

When I woke up
in your parents' bed
with my wife at my side
while your family slept
scattered around the house
the light beaming through
the windows was so sharp
and clear it was as if
I could see not only
out far but in deep.

I knew we had been
given a place to sleep
that was a position
of honor and a manifestation

of spirit so large and generous
I felt honor and humility
mixed with shame.

I saw on the white walls
beautifully composed
photographs of you,
your sisters and brothers
and nieces and nephew
framed in light wood
that set off your dark hair,
mocha skin, and luminous
ebony eyes with a simplicity
that was powerful,
eloquent and awesome

and the love
and pride
and dignity
and sense of
immeasurable wealth
and gratitude
were so pure
and palpable
in the bedroom
where I had been
given to sleep
I became choked
with salty grief

over the realization
that we who came
later from elsewhere
to this beautiful
land and landscape
have not had
the eyes to see,
the ears to listen,

the hearts to feel,
the wisdom to understand
what was here
and still remains

and could help us
become the people
we must be
to walk in dignity
and beauty
and balance

and a strength
that speaks not
with a big stick
but a large heart
and deep spirit.

8. Maggie's Hands

While your father
and I sat talking
before the cedar
that burned
in the makeshift
metal grill that sat
above sandy ground
I saw your mother
lift an ax and split
more cedar in two
and put it on the fire

and when the cedar
had burned down
to embers and ash
I watched her
scoop a handful

of dough from
the bowl I held,
shape it into a ball,
pat it and punch it,
twirl it and shape it
and flatten it and plop
it on the sizzling
grill and begin
the process anew,

reach down later
with a bare hand
to flip the doughy
disk over to
the other side,

and when one was
done lift it with
the same hand
and flip it into
the bigger bowl
I now held
as the heat increased
and my load of fresh
steaming bread grew
heavier in my hand,

and when I tore
off a piece at her
command and took
a bite and felt warm
Navajo tortilla
settle on my tongue
like the bread of life,

I knew Maggie's
sure hands had shaped
and touched you with love

and finished you into
the beautiful young
woman who walked into
my life and the embrace
of my family

and whose hands
will touch a man
and children in
the right way

and hold and move
a pen so that what
flows from it will
nourish and uplift
those to come.

9. Maggie's Gift

When I wear
the turquoise necklace
your mother gave to me
in gratitude for cultivating
the gift for words
and love of tradition
you received from her
and your father
while I listened,
looked on, and asked
a question or two,

the sun darkens
the skin on the back
of my neck and face,
my step has a little
more spring, I look more
handsome in the mirror

as I begin to resemble
the singer George Strait,
Maggie's beloved hero,
and the song I sing
sounds at least as good
as his greatest hits.

10. Your Father's Gift

When your father
tells you stories
about the elders
and their sacred ways
he is passing on
to someone whose heart
is open what comes
through him and who
he knows will carry on
the life of the spirit.

I have sat next to
him in the evening
outside the new home
he decades later received
as compensation in another
part of Navajoland and heard
the sad story of how his family
lost to the Hopis the farm
in the mountains where they
had lived for generations,

and I have sat next to him
beside a cedar fire over which
you mother would later bake
tortillas and heard your father
admit that after his illness
he looked in the mirror

and came to realize why
his children began to see
him as an old man though
he is almost a decade
younger than I,

and at that moment
I understood why he
had told me when he
was a guest in our house
that when we grow old our
children become our guides,

and I knew from
watching his proud
and dignified face
and listening to his
words of wisdom

that he appreciates
the great gift
of a dark-eyed daughter
whose beauty of spirit
he has seen deepen
and which will be
passed on to others
in the stories she
shall continue to tell.

11. Outside of Time

Hugging is good medicine
and when we come together
to touch to say goodbye
for now your breathing
and mine begin to merge
and the whole universe

is one slow rhythm
and what could have kept
us apart in the past
or even the present
dissolves and two traditions
have found a way to speak
to one another without
words with feeling that
pulls spirit to the center
and I hold you like a daughter
who is sweetheart and this
slow beat of heart and pulse
of blood blesses all we
have learned to share
and cultivate and when time
enters back into the equation
of what we give and take
the skin of my lips touches
yours and I step back from
the calm and curve of what
you are and who you shall
become as dawn slides
away from dark and things
take shape and consecrate
this world we have found
ourselves to be a part of.

12. Beyond Dark Eyes

Beyond your dark eyes
that give off light but do
not admit easy entry
I have felt strength
of spirit passed down
from those who came before,
reverence for a way
of life your heart

and hands will keep alive,
and a love of the word
as sacred power that will
heal anyone who has
the faith to believe
in the light that shines
in your dark eyes.

13. Rejoicing Song for Emma Danielle Roman Nose

As the nights grew longer
and Gaudete Sunday approached
we waited for the light
to appear again in our life
as the snow fell deep
and the world seemed to stop
and the voice of one crying
in the desert reminded us
to testify to the one who will
come as light into our life,

and you came
and your cry was a miracle
coming from so far away
and the world was stilled
with snow piled all around
and the line of your black
hair and the depth of your dark
Diné, Cheyenne, and Arapaho eyes
and the flesh of your lips
as you lay in your mother's
arms and looked up toward
your father looking down
at you appeared on the screen
as if by a magic sent us
from spirits far beyond

and I wept tears of joy
at this vision come from afar
and we gathered together
to look at you and your mother
and your father and we gave
thanks and rejoiced for the light
that you cast on us and the world.

5. Full Moon over Central Indiana

Calling on Ma Rainey

Many doors open, Ma,
sooner or later, when you bring
the right heart and know what to do.
You came back home to this house
in Columbus, Georgia, after your
song wound down. Though the hour
was late, we rang the bell and waited.
We knew you were there. My heart
beat like a brush on the skin
of a drum waiting for the voice
of a Blues Mama to kick off a song.

Your door opened, Ma,
and a young woman named Kisha
smiled at us and said,
"We ain't open here yet, but I'm
mo let you in." Kisha never stopped
smiling while we were in your house.

She put you on a jukebox
that learned how to read a CD
and my heart beat to the sounds
of your bluesy, jazzy, gut-bucket soul.
Yeah, the "Oh Papa Blues."
Yeah, "Ma Rainey's Black Bottom."
Yeah, "Screech Owl Blues"
in the middle of the night,
though the evening sun still shone
in the hot Georgia skies.
"Don't Fish in My Seas,"
you called from the bedroom.

Kisha showed us your quartered oak bed,
all done up proud, dark grain glowing.
Showed us the mantel on the fireplace

in which your fire still burned when
you got into bed and gazed at flames.
Showed us your pearls hanging
on the oval mirror of your oak dresser,
your hat pins resting in a ceramic holder.
I heard you sing "Booze and Blues"
as I looked into the mirror and saw
your face grin knowingly back at me.
Kisha showed us you are everywhere
in your house, Gertrude Pridgett.

I sat on the stool in front of your piano
and heard your "Farewell Daddy Blues,"
but there is no farewell for someone
who sings the blues like you, Gertrude.

Across the street from the projects,
in the expanse of Porterdale Cemetery,
we found your shiny new tombstone
calling you "Mother of the Blues,"
above the flat slab on the ground
which first marked your passing.

Doors open when anyone sings the blues
like you sang the blues, Ma Rainey.
Some hearts be closed, some be open,
some still got to learn how to open.
We came, yeah, and you were at home.
You made us welcome in the house
you built with blues. We say thanks.
We say you live always, you are in this
American house for all time, we hear you
always when Bessie and all your sisters
and daughters sing the great American blues.

Bessie's Business

Bessie's business was to sing the blues whole
from the bottom of her tough-mama soul.

Bessie sang the blues like a mean mama
who took no nonsense from any papa.

When Bessie bent her notes low and blue,
you knew she was starin' straight at you.

When Bessie sang her world-weary soul-bottom blues,
any aggrivatin' daddy felt a tightenin' of the screws.

When Bessie asked you to please come home,
you knew it was way past time for you to roam.

If Bessie sang the bitter old bed bug blues,
you felt your sorry soul ooze outta your shoes.

If Bessie sang you were making her your fool,
you knew you'd been unforgivably cruel.

When Bessie sang from the bottom of her soul,
the power of her blues could make you whole.

How Billie Sings the Blues

Oh Billie, oh Baltimore baby,
nobody sings the blues like you.

They say your range was limited,
but your voice travels hundreds
of miles of pain, able to wear
out countless pairs of shoes.

In your voice, I hear
light years of feeling,
see colors of emotions
in so many shades and nuances
you make me see my heart
was color blind until
I fell for sweet, sad you.

Oh Billie, oh Baltimore baby,
nobody sings the blues like you.

You crawl inside Solitude
and make us feel we live
there on the inside with you,
your lamp of love turned down low
but giving us just enough warmth.
You bend the slow dark notes
till they come back bruised
a spiritual black and blue.

You took a poem by a teacher
about a lynching and make us
witness the foul injustice
of what we do to one another
by using your quiet voice
to register so intensely
the horror of our inhumanity

that it explodes in our faces
and we find our hands coming
together for you, you, you.

Oh Billie, oh Baltimore baby,
nobody sings the blues like you.

On the Road with
the Hampton Sisters

Virtue is too frail to slap the bass
and so she stays seated and beats time
on her thighs until Aletra takes off
West to get her kicks on Route 66

and so Virtue, who cannot be left behind,
stands up to the mic and sings along
and the Hampton Sisters are on the road again,
as they were with the Family seventy years ago,

when towns closed to them at dusk
and restaurants and hotels would not open,
but they persisted and they endured,
and now they are singing for us all,

black, brown, white, yellow, red,
and they know the lay of this land
and the topography of the heart
and the geography of the soul,

and their spirit soars unstoppable,
they are both timely and timeless,
inside time and outside time,
carry us with them wherever they go,

and Aletra tells us them that's got shall
get and them that's not got shall lose,
and now Billie's on the road with us too,
and the Sisters tell us what Mama and Papa

may have is one thing, but what God
blesses is the child that's got his own,
and we know now these Sisters have
got their own, and what they got they give

to us, and we are rich and blessed because
we are lucky enough to be here to receive
what God gave us, which is Virtue and Aletra
and soul and spirit and spunk and love galore.

What Have You Gone and Done?

for Monika Herzig

Monika, Monika,
what have you
gone and done?

You came here
from somewhere else
and showed us
with your pianist's fingers
how to listen to the music
that is pulsing in our veins.

You set Louie Armstrong's
trumpet free to blow
us back to New Orleans
and points way beyond.
We heard and followed
the procession in the streets
and tasted a great gumbo
of musical styles and flavors
that stay on the tongue
and smack on the lips.

You had trumpeter Wynton
of New Orleans tell us
why we already love
what we didn't know
was ours all along.

Monika, Monika
what have you
gone and done?

You came to Indiana

from Swabia via Alabama
and brought us home
to an Indiana Avenue
no longer visible to the eye
but still alive in the sound
of Wes Montgomery's
soulful octaves guitar,
Melvin Rhyne's boogie-woogie
organ in the background,
Everett Greene's alluvial deep voice,
J.J. Johnson's note-bending slide trombone,
Freddy Hubbard's blister-lips trumpet,
Pookie Johnson's sweet-soul saxophone.

You told us about
the Hampton Sisters dressed
in their Sunday best singing
down South and in Harlem
and coming back home to Indiana
with Virtue slapping the bass
and Aletra singing, from the bottom
of a soul that only goes deeper
as she grows older, lyrics from
the treasure trove of memory.

Monika, Monika
what have you
gone and done?

You showed us it don't mean a thing
if it ain't got that swing,
you brought us Bessie and Billie,
Ella and Sarah and Diana,
the Duke and the Count and Benny,
and Bebop Bird and Coltrane
and Miles' many incarnations.

You led us to the Chatterbox

down Massachusetts Avenue,
brought Cole and Hoagy
alive with your fingertips,
asked us with a smile
to name that familiar tune,
and needled us, with just
the right kind of German sass:
"Come on, its your heritage!"

Monika, Monika
what have you
gone and done?

You laid a flatted fifth
in our ears, let us see
that jazz is beneath our feet
as we walk these streets
and in this American air
as we breathe and the music
will never stop as long
as one heart beats.

Song for Cassandra Wilson

I saw a woman sing the blues
from the bottom of her sultry
Delta soul. When she sang,
Lord, she moved like the earth,
seasons turned in her fluid hips,
her eyes gave off light from far
beyond, and the band followed
her snapping fingers like birds
swooping to the ground for seed.

This Mississippi woman could
be kitten, purring and meowing
for her lover to come back home,
she could give both sass and sob,
she could tell the mighty men
who ran the world where they
had gone dead wrong and how
they better fix it real quick or else
Mama's door would slam shut loud.

This woman named Cassandra
sang the blues, she sang jazz,
she sang a mean country heartbreak,
she rocked out like a roadhouse
on a jumpin' Saturday night.

When the show was over
she stood there in a pool
of blue light, bowed to us,
put fingertips to sensual lips,
blew us a kiss that brought us her love,
our beautiful husky-voiced queen
of the Mississippi day and night.

When Diana Sings Cole

When Diana sings Cole,
the clock stops ticking,
traffic fades into oblivion,
I go far away with her.

We walk along the Seine.
It's neither night nor day,
but some time in between,
before birds begin to sing.

When Diana sings Cole,
she gets under my skin,
leads me into lunar light
glowing in her golden hair.

Along the Seine, she turns
and sings sultry lyrics
in a voice that descends
deep into heart and soul.

When Diana sings Cole,
my world stops turning;
I wake up at dawn on the bank
of the River Mississenewa.

Standing in an Indiana town
with Diana's voice in my ear
and Cole's words on my tongue,
I lift this song with the birds.

Song for Lucinda Williams

Sing, bittersweet sister, grounded
in earth but scanning the skies.

Sing your sultry mix of country and blues.
Sing of heartbreak and hurt, southern and slow.

Smolder in your lush sensuality
that flames up again when warm

breezes blow under Louisiana sun,
moss sways on the live oaks,

and love of the right man or place
rubs and strikes the old match.

Sing for us your song as pure
as sugar cane on the tongue

and sea salt raw in the wound.
You are the daughter still looking

and listening in the back seat,
tires crunching on the gravel road,

as the family moves again from
one place to the next. Your wide

open eyes and ears register
lives taken and loves lost

but celebrate the joy of staying
put in this sweet old world,

the only one we can caress.
Now as you drive under stars

down the dark lost highway,
memory is your muse, longing

is your subject, and your gift
is to name and measure the space

between the earth we know
and a heaven we crave.

Song for Carrie Newcomer

after a 9/11 memorial concert

As the dusk thickened,
I read as a boy in the upstairs
bedroom beside a sugar maple.

The song of the doves
started in the spruces
at the back of the garden.

Their quiet cooing lifted
from evergreen branches
and drifted soft and low

telling of things to come
I could not see, and their
song lodged in my psyche.

I hear it still wherever
I am when dark approaches,
for song so deep we carry

with us wherever we go.
Now the dove becomes
an Indiana folksinger whose

dusky alto speaks
to my deepest ear and tells
of a daughter whose father

would always walk with her
through whatever dark
would come her way.

The song of the dove
leads her to a stand of
spruces where a community

of spirits gathers like
a congregation of listeners
whose minister prepares

to speak, but what comes
out of his opening mouth
is dove song that is alto,

a lyric of love speaking
for a community
of souls gathered one

by one and two by two
in a diner in southern
Indiana that is also

a church and an auditorium
where as dusk descends
the deep song of the dove

cooing in the branches
of a spruce behind a garden
is the lyric of an Indiana

folksinger whose song
comes to us as one voice
for all, rich or poor,

white or black, red
or brown, one color,
one religion, one spirit.

Baby Blue

It wasn't that the time had
come for us to tear apart.

There was no orphan crying
like a fire in the mid-day sun.

There was no great kiss-off,
no one-up exchange of good-byes.

Her eyes were baby blue,
mine were earth brown,

we were two planets
that had spun together

and revolved around one
another intensely for a time.

Then her star had to shine
elsewhere, my planet knew

where to stay put, and we
both knew it was all over.

But I still love the baby blue
I sometimes see across the sky

and hope she likes to touch
the earth on the path she walks.

The Other Side

for Katherine

My father's waters were sometimes troubled
and my mother would try to keep them calm.
Sometimes she was our bridge to the other side.

My waters are sometimes troubled
and you try your best to keep them calm.
Sometimes you are my bridge to the other side.

Your waters are sometimes troubled
and I try my best to keep them calm.
Sometimes I am your bridge to the other side.

When a woman plays a piano,
sometimes she tries to keep us calm,
sometimes she tries to stir us up,

and whenever she lets her fingertips go,
she takes us beyond where we have ever been,
and she is our bridge to the other side.

Full Moon over Central Indiana

for Kriss Luckett-Ziesemer and Greg Ziesemer

In the light of a full moon
over Carmel, Indiana, we sit
at a table in the open air as fresh

breezes touch and re-touch our skin
and a man and woman, standing
as if they are right where

they want to be in the universe,
sing in sensual harmony a song
about "Sweet Sister Moon."

His voice and guitar lend perfect
support to her words about
tucking the moon's power

in her back pocket for a rainy
night. On this June night
when no raindrops fall and all

the elements of weather and song
and men and women and words
and rhythm blend into harmony,

for once everything comes together
as we wish it would, all is sweet,
round, complete as a circle and as

full as bright sister moon, nothing
needs to be translated, and all hearts
participate in one universal beat.

6. Her Circle

Facets

Sometimes she's a sister,
sometimes a daughter,

and whoever's a daughter
is half a sweetheart.

Sometimes she's a mother,
sometimes a healer,

sometimes she's a visionary
who sings a prophetic song,

sometimes she sings of love,
sometimes she sings of loss,

sometimes her voice is throaty,
sometimes it's shrill.

Sometimes she's a madwoman,
sometimes the voice of reason.

Sometimes she's a child of the earth,
sometimes a daughter of the ether.

When she speaks in any
of the voices she commands,

she masters the art of saying
more than mortal words suggest.

Sometimes she's an advisor
in various kinds of campaigns,

sometimes she leads the troops away,
sometimes she calls them back home,

sometimes she chides,
sometimes she consoles,

she knows how to draw out the best
and make it look like it's your least.

Always she's human,
on occasion sounds divine,

at times these spheres separate, spin
apart, come back together, unite as one.

Whenever she becomes a lover
she acts as all these at once,

mother, sister, daughter,
dancer, singer, voluptuary,

instructs you in the art of when
and how to move, when to stay still;

and when you've been one
with her and look into her eyes

you know she has seen well
beyond what you think you are

and what you want to become
though she says not one word

as she relaxes her hold on you
and goes back to where you

thought she was before she took
you beyond where you've ever been.

Follower

I have followed your markings
on trees others could not see.
Now I enter your secret cave
where air is moist and warm.
Like the wicks of candles,
your eyes glow in their recesses.
Now and then a summer breeze
stirs the darkness between us.
When I hold my breath,
I feel your fallow flesh
rise like a fertile field
to spring rain, then fall.
When your soft voice tongues
my name in sensual music
that swells and lies in my ears,
I take bold steps toward you.
Blood rises to every surface.
I come to be at your service.

Aphrodisiac

Better than oil
of herbs and spices
that scent the skin
is good talk that
opens eyes and ears.

Better than potions
concocted in the night
to sip and enlarge
the libido is talk
that rises from
the depths of soul
and spreads like
blood through
the system to tingle
in fingertip and toe.

Better than words
contrived and sold
for the occasion
is talk that wells up
from within and must
be shared between
man and woman

and opens them to
one another
pulls them down
to the depths
making them ache
for the touch of flesh
and the coming together
of two whole
beings as one.

Love Letter

You ask if the shoulder
joint the medicine man
scoped could bear
the pain of your love.

Have I not been
your faithful warrior
on all of love's
battle fields?

If earthly pain
be the wages
of your divine love,
come down to
my level, make me
pay, pay, pay.

Let us light
all the candles
in your grotto.

Deep and dark one,
give me, give me
all the earthly pain,
all the divine love
that you got!

Love Prayer

May our skin
touch in as
many places
and ways
as possible.

Children's Story

When the well-known poet
came to read and talk
about the ways of life
of his people, his wife,

a fine but less known poet,
walked quietly in his shadow.
With a smile, she carried his
child with beauty and grace.

The children listened
to the poet read his poems
filled with passion and mystery,
but they followed the mother

of his child wherever she stepped.
They knew that to carry yourself
and a life to come in beauty is
the kind of poem all must read.

Song from Darkness

In a poem this voice I hear
as mine can say things
to you from a part of the self
that must be kept down
in darkness during daylight

so I rise from the radiant
darkness of dream to say
to you, my friend, voice
that has whispered in my ear,

that no man, be he CEO,
soldier, picture maker,
wordsmith or wandering
wailer of hobo song,

no man may tie the tongue
of a woman he loves
without exposing himself
to a lashing from the elements

and the woman who gives
birth to a son can also give
birth to song and when her
tongue unties itself and sings
this song that comes to her
from the depths of her past
and explodes into the present
with all the power of her
life-giving sensual gift,

then all creatures of two
and four legs stop to listen
and look for the sacred sayer
they had not known walked
in balance in their midst.

Dirty Blues

When a man, whether
ditch digger or poet,

or both, loves a woman,
whether goddess, human,

or both, it is good
that he put his hands

on her in the right way
to move her and make her moan;

but whether he is pacifist
or warrior, if that man

clench his fist and strike
the woman he loves

making her holy flesh
swell to black and blue,

the gods and the mortals
and birds and beasts in the forest

cry out together in shame
against this abuse of nature

and sing the low down dirty blues
until someone comes forth

to touch gentle lips
to the spot on her flesh

where love's wound festers
because blood turned so dark.

Her Circle

We sit in a circle
to talk about the oral
tradition in Native poetry

and our guest, whose
Lenape ancestors
lived in this region

ages before our families
arrived from other lands,
asks for volunteers

to read passages from
a Zuni narrative
in which the community

remembers the ancestors
and gives praise by
naming plants and animals.

Soon she calls
her devotees by name,
they respond to her

questions, she lowers
her voice to a near
hush to make

a point about contrast
and emphasis,
and everyone looks up

as her voice goes down.
I close my eyes and
imagine we are gathered

in a circle in a cave
around a campfire,
members of a religion

that has been around
since smoke rose from
the first flame ignited

by humans of their
own power, and we
listen to the words

of this woman
whose voice holds
us together in prayer.

Arboretum Naming Song

for Jeanetta Calhoun Mish

1
We cannot remain
in love with what
we cannot name

and because on this
October day when air
is crisp and sunlight
so clear we do not
want to risk falling
out of love with this
world into which
we were born
no matter how
bruised it may be

we come from different
places and traditions
to stand, to see, to say:

Thundercloud Plum,
burgundy leaves
stirring in the breeze;

Tabletop Scotch Elm,
grainy bark climbing stem,
smooth bark stretching
across tabletop branches
above a seam where
grafted skins touch;

Blue Atlas Cedar,
blue-gray needles

falling light
as snowflakes
to Paumanok ground
far from mountains
in African home.

We look, we read, we say,
we lay hands on ancient trunk;
what we feel lies beyond
palms, fingertips and words.

2
We walk through a formal garden
where late roses bloom,
into a woods where chipmunks
chip and squirrels scamper.

What we see comes
to us so fast we step
outside ourselves, untie
our tongues and let them
sing praise to what stands
on either side of us like
familiar spirits happy
to have their names
on this earth invoked:

White Oak, Red Oak, you say.
Scarlet Oak, Black Oak, I reply.

Black Locust, Tulip Poplar, you sing.
Red Maple, Sugar Maple, I answer.

Sweet Gum, you chant.
Black Birch, I conclude.

Children of the Morning Star

We sit cross-legged
on the earth, in the skin,
facing one another
under the light
of the morning star,
children of Venus.

The woods are quiet,
birds have not
yet begun to sing
their pre-dawn hymn
from branches above.

What burns in our eyes
we reflect to one another
in this sacred moment
as it comes to us
from the star above.

Our pores could
not be open wider
to one another.

First you recite
a poem no one
has ever heard.
I nod, give you
another nobody
has ever heard.

Where these holy
hymns come from
is the star above,
beacon of love.

One day we shall
pass these songs on
to children who follow,
but for now we
do not yearn for
the heat of the sun,
the light of day,
any time to come.

We sit cross-legged
on the earth, in our skin,
in these quiet woods
facing one another
outside of time
and bask in the light
of Venus, children
of the morning star.

7. Songs of Helga: After Andrew Wyeth

Songs of Helga: After Andrew Wyeth

1. Helga Asleep

In the beginning of the universe
there were rays of darkness

shooting toward one
full buttock moon risen

to the level of a long pedestal
on which she lay curled,

and the shadows were
aroused in all quarters

to crawl toward every
crevice they could find.

2. To Awaken Her

When you walk
in the door

she sits up
abruptly
between sheets

with a look
half surprise,
half relief,

and her pigtails
brush the falling
breasts giving off

the shapeliest shadows
anyone could touch.

3. In the Flesh

When she lies on her back
on the earth beneath a tree,
green leaf shadows
play on her breasts,

and the brown patch
between her legs

stands out like
moss in sunlight

that has found
the right place

to lie down
and doze.

4. In Sheepskin

It's not the way the sheepskin
circles her wrists making a V

from the breastbone up to her
shoulder or the way it flares

around the bottom of the coat
opened at the right angle

on the side away from us,
or the long hair tinged

with the betrayal of age
having its own will as it

falls nearly to where the V opens
onto the mauve wool sweater,

with turtle-neck almost touching
the shapely chin, or the ripe-peach

red on the right cheek and the bridge
of the nose, or the arching of her

legs into the black boots that
disappear with a slight swerve

into the bottom right corner. No,
it's the look in those eyes turned

on a part of the floor we cannot see
and the disposition of the hands

as they bend together, one enclosing
the other, as the long thumbs

with dirt beneath their
nails cross one another,

at just the right angle,
in just the right place.

5. She Daydreams

As she lies in bed on her side,
right hand holding the lower left arm,

she is all curve and slope and shape
in a world as white as melting snow,

155

and a breeze all the way from the Baltic
blows through twin windows at her back,

lifting sheer lace curtains over
her and her bed in broad daylight,

sailing her and her vessel of flesh
across the dark waters of dream.

6. On Her Knees

Even in this position
in bed she's never

been known to beg.
She turns her head

so the sunlight
is forced to settle

on the strands of hair
that whirlpool down

into a russet pigtail.
One hand turns

behind to rest,
near the wrist,

on an invisible cheek
as the ends of knotted

pigtails turn and twist
competing with nipples.

All she offers is

an eyelash pulling

a lid almost
over an eye.

7. She Walks in Leaves

When she walks alone
like a Prussian Alice

in autumn woods, her head
is but a flicker of light

surrounded by burnished
maple leaves sunk to

the forest floor and swollen
as large as the sails

of the ship on which her
grandparents came to America.

8. In Moonlight

Turned on her side
in front of
the farmhouse window,

with her eyes closed
as the darkness
and a small waterfall
serenade her sleep,

she raises her right
arm across her head
and over the pillow,

and the sheet falls
to where the short
hair curls.

As she dreams
of a man she loves,
her mouth mimes
a rocking rhythm,

and moonlight blesses
her left nipple

and the side
of the mound
with the navel
in the middle.

9. On Her Back

When she lies on her back
in rust and brown leaves

in the fir-green Loden coat,
her braid is the limp tail

of a creature of the forest
come to rest in the haven

of her warm chest, the late
winter sun pouring into her

eyes draws the back of her
right wrist to her forehead,

her eyelids droop into shadow,
and thoughts turn in the back

of her mind like a snake
just beginning to uncoil.

10. Seen from Behind

As she removes the hands
crossed behind her back

against her buttocks,
she swings her arms

forward as she tiptoes
into the darkness

as if testing the coolness
of surf at her feet.

The small of her back
collects a puddle of shadow,

the darkness surges up
her legs like a tide,

and breasts float
loose in the waves.

11. In Braids

There is sun on her face
and wind on her lips

and fire in the hair
wrapped around her head.

Gray clouds scud across

blue sky in her sweater.

Feel the warmth of late
summer afternoon in the twists

of hair that fall toward
the swelling of her breasts

like the wild grapevines
a boy has been swinging

on and lets go of as he
splashes into the pond.

12. Queen of May

Maybe it's spring
and those are green leaves
and white flowers
crowning her fair head,

but the long hair
that makes an oval
of the baby-soft skin
of her curved face

is the burnt gold
of the harvest.

Maybe she's just come
from the decking
of the village maypole,

maybe she's just danced
with the lord of May
and sipped a ceremonial glass
of May wine tinged

with the flavor
of *Waldmeister,*

but you'd have to
step out of the shadows,
put your hand
on her shoulder,

and taste the sweet
woodruff on her
lips with yours

to make this queen
who looks so royal
against everything
that is dark

lift her blue
eyes to yours,

open up
and whisper

that what she loves
most is seeing
off in the distance

what's now green
slowly turn
to gold, rust,
and crimson,

fall and
then re-
turn

to good
brown earth.

13. Seated by a Tree

She is alone but not alone
as she snuggles in the shadows

against the base of the huge tree
with the rough bark in a space

between gnarled roots. As her
ruddy hair swerves across her face

and a speck of sunlight shows
the green moss at home on the bark,

what we know is that this
goddess of American earth

is at one with every
single thing around her.

14. In Black Velvet

When she stretches out on her back
in the dark, legs crossed at the ankles,

head turned away so we can't see
her face, breasts spread out,

the hair brushing her neck
a flame flickering in the night,

a patch of sunset red fuzz aglow
on the triangle between her legs,

the illuminated body stretched
out and floating in the dark

with a strip of black velvet
around her neck tethering her

to the darkness, it is hard to tell
if she is pure form or perfect flesh.

15. What She Recalls When
She Sits for a Painting

The faraway look in her mother's
blue eyes as her life faded away,

the sparkle of the golden angel
perched atop the Christmas tree
in the living room
when she was a little girl,

the sting on her behind
when her father whipped her
for spilling a canister
of fresh warm milk
onto frozen earth,

the splatter in the slop bucket
in the middle of winter nights
and the aroma as it brewed
under the bed until first light,

her daughter's first cry
when the midwife
slapped her to life,

and the pain that tore
at her gut when the child
burned at the forehead

coughing and crouping
through the night
throwing up on sheets,

the squall of tires as they
caught on the asphalt road
after the teenage son spun rocks
in the barnyard fishtailing
toward town on a Saturday night
barely making it home in time
for Sunday morning milking,

the desire she could not choke
as she gave herself the first time
to the man who said he would
spend the rest of his life with her,

the warnings her mother
gave as they kneaded dough
about men who made promises
and broke them in the next breath,

the first time her daughter
asked her how to make babies,

the stories her grandmother told
in German, as she sat on her lap,
of the Prussian village where
church bells pealed or tolled
every day every quarter of an hour,

and the manure pile steamed
winter mornings just outside
the door of the farmhouse
where relatives might still live,
and the little graveyard across
the road where the family name
was carved in the old script

on tomb after tomb,

and whether she could speak
German with any of the people
with her mother's maiden name
if she ever had the chance
to visit the Old Country,

and how it would feel
to hold a grandchild
in her arms the first time

and what the world
would be like by the time
her grandchild turned twenty-one
if everything kept changing
as fast as it has changed
since she was a little girl,

and whether she would still
want to be alive then.

16. Behind Drawn Shades

She is in league with the darkness.
In this still room they conspire.
You can hear them breathe together.

Even when she pulls her hair
back to the side just above the ear
to make herself severe

it slithers behind and reappears
around the other shoulder

and slides down to the breast
resting against a folded arm.

Because she looks away
you are sure she has
hidden an apple
somewhere in this room.

How to get the first bite?

17. Seated on a Stool

She sits on a stool
in the darkness
near the window
where she once let
her hair fall down.

She is the light
in the room.

She is younger
than she was
the day you met.

Her face turns
away again, but
nothing else.

The rest of her
turns, conscious
or not, toward
someone nearby.

A small oval
of light from
the world beyond

has found her

left nipple,

another large
triangle cuts
across one hip
toward the other knee,

highlighting a few
brown curlicues
from the smaller
triangle between
her legs.

You want to touch
your lips to the
flecks of light

at her left ankle
where her legs cross
on the stool

and the base
of her neck
where the skin
stretches tight.

18. Walking on a Country Road

The only light
in the whole scene
of muddy brown
flecked with red
falls on the back
of her head

where the hair

streaked with gray

pulls tight
into braids.

Before you reach
the five evergreens

on the horizon
you want to

step up and
kiss the nape

of her neck
before she dis-

appears over the
side of the hill.

19. Against a Tree in Winter

She and the expanse of bark
she leans back against
are almost one.

Her hands snuggle
in the pockets of
the Loden coat.

Heel and sole
of her right boot
are propped on a rock
half a step away.

Light snow streaks

the brown hillside
beyond woman and tree.

Everything is frozen.
Everything is dead.
She is alone.

Her pale Nordic face
is the only light.

The whole story
can never be told.

About the Author

Indiana Poet Laureate Norbert Krapf is a native of Jasper, Indiana, a German community. He received his B.A. from St. Joseph College (Indiana) and his M.A. and Ph.D. in English from the University of Notre Dame. After thirty-four years of teaching at Long Island University, where he directed the C.W. Post Poetry Center, he moved with his family to Indianapolis in 2004.

Since then he has published the poetry collections *Looking for God's Country* (Time Being Books, 2005); *Invisible Presence: A Walk through Indiana in Photographs and Poems* (Indiana Univ. Pr., 2006), with Darryl Jones; *Bloodroot: Indiana Poems* (Indiana Univ. Pr., 2008), with b/w photographs by David Pierini; a prose memoir, *The Ripest Moments: A Southern Indiana Childhood* (Indiana Historical Society Pr., 2008), with 74 period photographs; and a CD with jazz pianist and composer Monika Herzig, *Imagine—Indiana in Music and Words* (Acme Records, 2007).

Krapf received the Lucille Medwick Memorial Award from the Poetry Society of America and serves on the board of Etheridge Knight, Inc., which brings the arts to those traditionally underserved. As IPL, he has a special interest in reuniting poetry and music. For more details, go to www.krapfpoetry.com

LaVergne, TN USA
25 February 2010
174222LV00004B/35/P